spot

SPORTS

TENNIS

by Mari Schuh

AMICUS | AMICUS INK

baseline

line umpire

Look for these words and pictures as you read.

racket

ball

A player serves.
The match begins.

The court has white lines. The ball must land inside the lines.

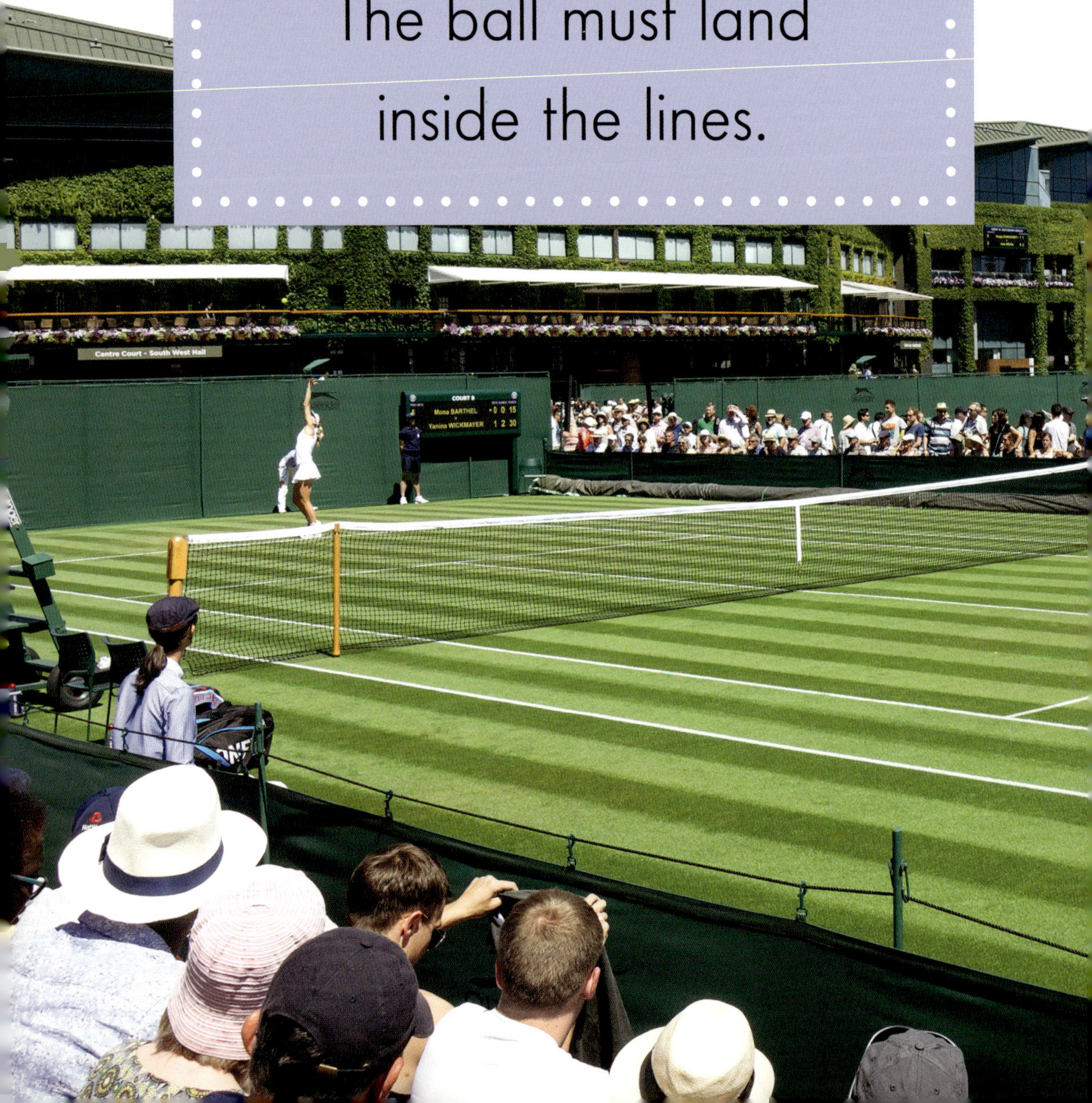

Do you see the baseline?
It is the back line.
A player serves there.

baseline

racket

Do you see the racket?
The round part is the head.

COURT NO. 3
PREVIOUS SETS
PLAYER
SETS
GAMES
POINTS
7 6
Robin SODERLING
2
5
6 4

Do you see the line umpire?
Is the ball in or out?
He says it is out!

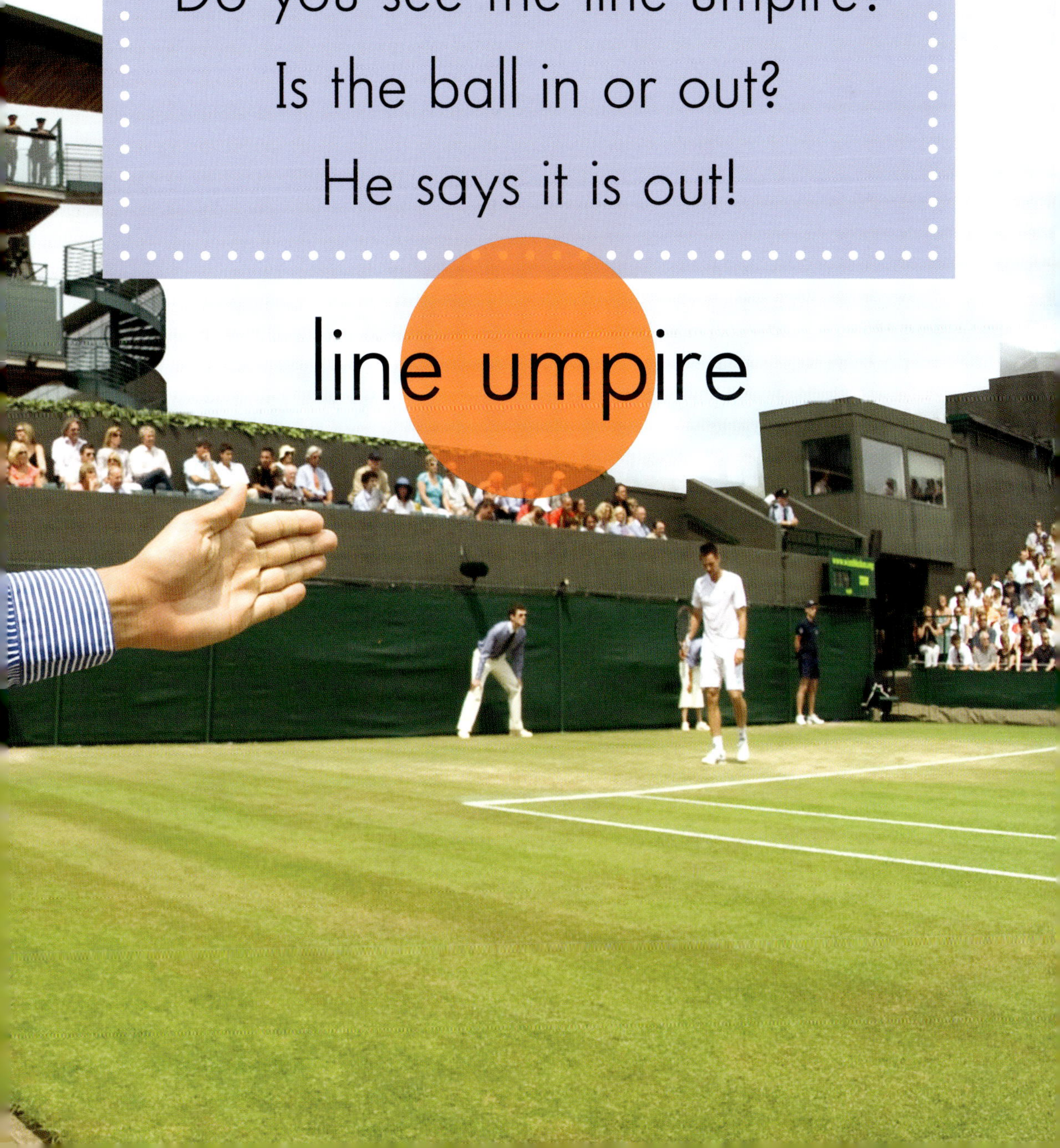

line umpire

ball

Do you see the ball?
Pow! It is hit high.
This shot is a lob.

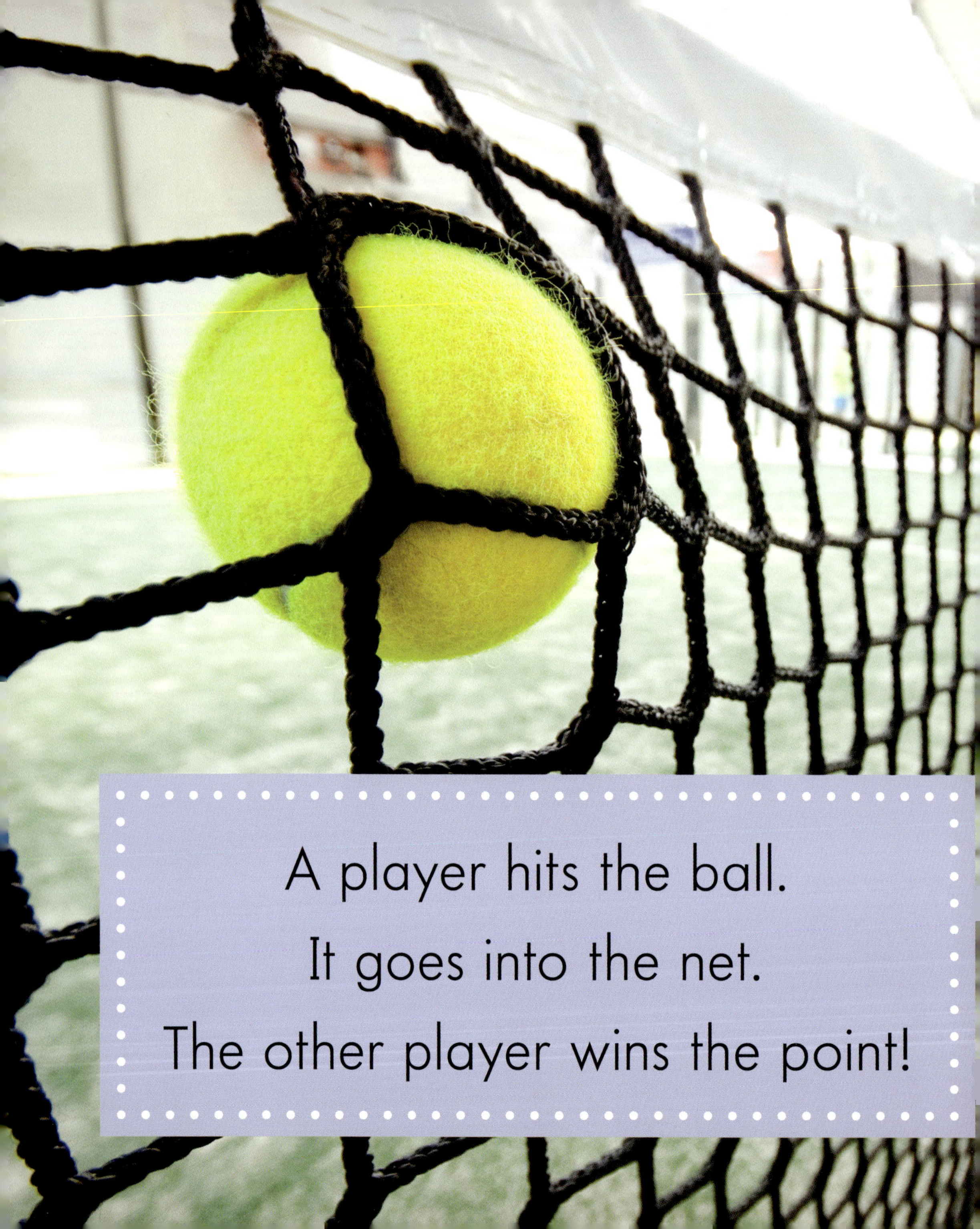

A player hits the ball.
It goes into the net.
The other player wins the point!

baseline

line umpire

Did you find?

racket

ball

Spot is published by Amicus and Amicus Ink
P.O. Box 1329, Mankato, MN 56002
www.amicuspublishing.us

Library of Congress Cataloging-in-Publication Data
Names: Schuh, Mari C., 1975- author. | Schuh, Mari C., 1975- Sports. | Amicus (Firm)
Title: Tennis / Mari C. Schuh.
Description: Mankato, Minnesota : Amicus, 2021. | Series: Spot. Sports | Audience: Ages 4-7 | Audience: Grades K-1 | Summary: "Elementary sports fans will ace key vocabulary in this high-interest leveled reader about the game of tennis. Simple text and color photos touch on basic equipment and rules"-- Provided by publisher.
Identifiers: LCCN 2019036312 (print) | LCCN 2019036313 (ebook) | ISBN 9781681519395 (Library Binding) | ISBN 9781681525860 (Paperback) | ISBN 9781645490241 (PDF)
Subjects: LCSH: Tennis--Juvenile literature. | Illustrated children's books. | Readers.
Classification: LCC GV996.5 .S36 2021 (print) | LCC GV996.5 (ebook) | DDC 796.342--dc23
LC record available at https://lccn.loc.gov/2019036312
LC ebook record available at https://lccn.loc.gov/2019036313

Printed in the United States of America

HC 10 9 8 7 6 5 4 3 2 1
PB 10 9 8 7 6 5 4 3 2 1

For Char —MS

Gillia Olson, editor
Deb Miner, series designer
Aubrey Harper, book designer and photo researcher

Photos by Alamy/Greg Balfour Evans 4–5, Imageplotter 3, Neil Tingle 10–11; AP/Adam Davy 12–13, Steven Paston 6–7; iStock/MaxRiesgo 14–15, OSTILL/cover, 1, 16, stanley45 8–9, stockcam cover (ball), 1, 3, 8, 12, 16